PANAMA 2016 HUMAN RIGHTS REPORT

EXECUTIVE SUMMARY

Panama is a multiparty constitutional democracy. In May 2014 voters chose Juan Carlos Varela Rodriguez as president in national elections that international and domestic observers considered generally free and fair. Varela assumed the presidency in July 2014.

Civilian authorities maintained effective control over the security forces.

The principal human rights problems were lengthy pretrial detention, harsh prison conditions marked by overcrowding, and widespread, low-level corruption, often practiced with impunity.

Other human rights problems included delayed court proceedings, including a judiciary susceptible to corruption and outside influence; violence against women and children; trafficking in persons; marginalization of indigenous people; societal discrimination based on HIV/AIDS status, sexual orientation, and disabilities; lengthy refugee processing; and child labor.

The Varela administration and the Public Ministry continued investigations into allegations of corruption against public officials.

Section 1. Respect for the Integrity of the Person, Including Freedom from:

a. Arbitrary Deprivation of Life and other Unlawful or Politically Motivated Killings

There were no reports the government or its agents committed arbitrary or unlawful killings.

b. Disappearance

There were no reports of politically motivated disappearances.

c. Torture and Other Cruel, Inhuman, or Degrading Treatment or Punishment

The constitution prohibits such practices, and there were no reports that government officials employed them.

Prison and Detention Center Conditions

Prison conditions remained harsh, due primarily to overcrowding, a shortage of prison guards, lack of adequate medical services, and inadequate sanitary conditions. There were no private detention facilities.

<u>Physical Conditions</u>: As of November the prison system, with an intended capacity of 14,174 inmates, held 17,165 prisoners. Pretrial detainees shared cells with convicted prisoners due to space constraints. Prison conditions for women were generally better than for men, but conditions for both populations remained poor, with overcrowded facilities, poor medical care, and a lack of basic supplies for personal hygiene. Some older facilities lacked potable water and adequate ventilation. There were no reports of inadequate lighting.

Juvenile pretrial and custodial detention centers also suffered from a lack of prison officials. There were 1,005 prison guards nationwide, including 176 new guards hired during the year, almost double the 547 guards in 2010. Officials estimated the system required 1,400 guards. In adult prisons, inmates complained of limited time outside cells and limited access for family members. Authorities acknowledged that insufficient Panama National Police (PNP) agent coverage limited exercise time for inmates on certain days.

In March, prompted by a motion filed before the Inter-American Human Rights Commission (IACHR), authorities transferred the six high-level gang leaders who were detained in the Punta Coco facility on a Pacific island to the Gran Joya complex on the mainland, leaving the facility vacant. Since Punta Coco's 2015 opening, human rights nongovernmental organizations (NGOs) had complained that there was no physician on the island; inmates could receive medical assistance only from the sole National Air Naval Service paramedic stationed there. In September, using public safety as a justification, President Varela ordered the transfer of four high-risk Chorrillo gang members to Punta Coco after they injured a child. The gang members' lawyer argued that the poor conditions of the detention center, including mosquito infestation, violated the detainees' human rights. They were transferred to a mainland prison in late November, leaving the facility vacant, and subsequently released pending trial.

The Human Rights Ombudsman's Office reported that the principal prisoner concern was poor or inadequate medical attention. Hypertension, diabetes, dermatitis, HIV/AIDS, tuberculosis, and respiratory illnesses were the most-common diseases among the prison population. Prison medical care was inadequate due to lack of personnel, transportation, and medical resources. As of August there were 73 medical staff (39 physicians, and 34 nurses and technical staff) assigned to all prisons nationwide. Authorities transferred patients with serious illnesses to public clinics, but there were difficulties arranging for the inmates' transportation. The penitentiary system did not have an ambulance; inmates were transported in police vehicles or in emergency services ambulances when available. As of September prison medical units continued to lack sufficient medicine. Authorities permitted relatives of inmates to bring medicine, although some relatives paid bribes to prison personnel, including PNP members, to bypass the required clearances.

As of October, 25 male inmates had died in custody. Twenty-one of these deaths resulted from chronic illnesses, including tuberculosis and HIV, and all but two occurred after inmates had been transferred to medical centers for attention. An additional four individuals died in prison from inmate-on-inmate violence.

Administration: The computerized system installed in 2015 to update and ensure accurate information on all inmates, including biographical data on inmates, their legal status, and information related to rehabilitation programs in which they participated, remained inaccessible to prosecutors at the Attorney General's Office, legal authorities of the judiciary, and the judicial investigative directorate within the National Police. During the year the penitentiary system's new Office for Special Projects installed more sophisticated software to allow interagency access, but as of August the software was not fully functional.

The penitentiary system continued to apply a policy of "two-for-one" reduction in time served, in which two days' work and/or study resulted in a one-day reduction in time remaining on the sentence. Prisoners could submit complaints to judicial authorities without censorship and request investigation of credible allegations of inhuman conditions, but authorities did not make the results of such investigations public. The Ombudsman's Office negotiated and petitioned on behalf of prisoners and received complaints about prison conditions. The Ombudsman's Office continued to conduct weekly prison visits to prisons in Panama City and Colon and, twice a year, to prisons elsewhere in the country. The government generally did not monitor its meetings with prisoners.

<u>Independent Monitoring</u>: The government permitted prison monitoring by independent nongovernmental observers. The Roman Catholic NGO Justice and Peace visited the two prisons in David, Chiriqui. The NGO reported overcrowding and corrupt behavior by prison officials, which included smuggled weapons, cigarettes, and cell phones for the inmates. Human rights NGOs wishing access to the prisons during fixed visiting hours must send a written request to the National Directorate of the Penitentiary System 15 days in advance.

<u>Improvements</u>: During the year the government reduced overcrowding at juvenile centers, including by employing alternatives to detention. The government also continued to transfer nonviolent prisoners to the La Nueva Joya complex; as of July, 2,283 inmates occupied 48 percent of the complex. By August authorities released 963 inmates throughout the penitentiary system due to sentence reductions and conditional releases. In September the president signed amendments to Law 42, which provides a career path for civilian prison officials, technicians, and administrative personnel within the National Directorate of the Penitentiary System.

In October, 139 prison inmates were the first beneficiaries of a higher learning partnership program between the prison system and Panamanian institutions of higher education.

During the year La Joyita's 60-bed clinic was remodeled and better equipped, although only available for limited hours.

d. Arbitrary Arrest or Detention

The law prohibits arbitrary arrest and detention, and the government generally observed these prohibitions.

Role of the Police and Security Apparatus

The country has no military forces. The PNP is principally responsible for internal law enforcement and public order. Civilian authorities in the Ministry of Public Security and the Ministry of the Presidency maintained effective control over all police, investigative, border, air, maritime, and migration services in the country. The government has mechanisms to investigate and punish abuse and corruption, but information on the process and results of investigations were rarely made public. Due to the lack of prison guards, the PNP was increasingly responsible for security both outside and inside of the prisons. Its leadership expressed concern over insufficient training and equipment.

Arrest Procedures and Treatment of Detainees

There were two judicial systems operating during the year, as the country completed its transition to an accusatory justice system in September, but cases opened prior to September 2 in the country's largest judicial districts (Panama, Colon, Darien, and Guna Yala continued to be tried under the old inquisitorial system.

Under the inquisitorial system, the prosecutor's office issues detention orders based on evidence. The law provides for suspects to be brought promptly before a judge. Lack of prompt arraignment continued to be a problem for cases tried under the old system; under the new system, a magistrate must arraign suspects expeditiously.

A functioning bail system existed for a limited number of crimes but was largely unused for most cases tried under the old system. Most bail proceedings are at the discretion of the Prosecutor's Office and cannot be independently initiated by detainees or their legal counsel.

The law requires arresting officers to inform detainees immediately of the reasons for arrest or detention and of the right to immediate legal counsel. Detainees gained prompt access to legal counsel and family members, and the government provided indigent defendants with a lawyer.

The law prohibits police from detaining adult suspects for more than 48 hours but allows authorities to detain minor suspects for 72 hours.

The preliminary investigation phase of detention under the old system lasted eight days to two months and the follow-up investigation phase lasted two to four months, depending on the number of suspects. In the new system, arrests and detention decisions are made on the basis of probable cause.

Pretrial Detention: The government regularly imprisoned inmates under the inquisitorial system for more than a year before a judge's pretrial hearing, and in some cases pretrial detention exceeded the minimum sentence for the alleged crime. As of July according to government statistics, 66 percent of prisoners were pretrial detainees. Some criticized the judiciary for applying unequal pretrial restrictive measures for individuals facing substantially similar charges.

Detainee's Ability to Challenge Lawfulness of Detention before a Court: Persons arrested or detained, regardless of whether on criminal or other grounds, are entitled to challenge in court the legal basis of arbitrary nature of their detention and obtain prompt release and compensation if found to have been unlawfully detained.

e. Denial of Fair Public Trial

While the law provides for an independent judiciary, the judicial system was inefficient and susceptible to corruption and outside influence, and faced allegations of manipulation by the executive branch.

During the year the judiciary hired 931 lawyers to serve as public defenders, judges, and magistrates under the new accusatory system; however, the NGO Pro-Justice Alliance and the National Bar Association complained that the Supreme Court did not comply with Law 53 of 2015, which establishes hiring practices and merit-based promotions in the judiciary. In addition, the NGO alleged that the new hires lacked independence, as some of them previously worked for current Chief Justice Jose Ayu Prado. The Supreme Court hired the 931 new employees on a "temporary" basis allegedly due to insufficient time and budget for permanent staff.

Trial Procedures

The law provides that all citizens charged with crimes enjoy the right to a presumption of innocence. They have the right to be informed promptly and in detail of the charges (with free interpretation as necessary for non-Spanish speaking inmates from the moment charged through all appeals), to a fair trial without undue delay, to counsel of their choice and adequate time and facilities to prepare a defense, to refrain from incriminating themselves or close relatives, and to be tried only once for a given offense. The accused may be present with counsel during the investigative phase of proceedings.

During the year the government completed the transition from an inquisitorial to an accusatory system of justice. In July the judiciary received 9.5 million balboas ($9.5 million) of the 20 million balboas ($20 million) requested in order to implement the new system, an amount the judiciary said, that only covered the salaries of newly hired justice employees, procurement of basic equipment, staff training, and facility costs. The Public Ministry received an additional 10 million balboas ($10 million) funding to implement its requirements under the new accusatory system of justice.

On September 2, the government implemented the accusatory system in the provinces of Panama (including the Special District of San Miguelito), Colon, Darien, and the Guna Yala, Wargandi, Madugandi, and Embera Wounnan comarcas (indigenous regions with a high degree of administrative autonomy). On September 3, a woman received a 60-month prison sentence for drug trafficking-- the first conviction under the accusatory system in Panama Province.

Under the accusatory system, trials are open to the public. Judges may order the presence of pretrial detainees for providing or expanding upon statements or for confronting witnesses. Trials are conducted based on evidence presented by the public prosecutor. Defendants have the right to be present at trial and to consult with an attorney in a timely manner. Defendants may confront or question adverse witnesses and present their own witnesses and evidence. Defendants and their attorneys have access to relevant government-held evidence. Defendants have a right of appeal. The law extends these rights to all citizens, and the judiciary generally enforced them.

The judiciary complained that many hearings were canceled due to inmates' failure to appear. The penitentiary system cited lack of sufficient PNP agents to transfer the inmates to the courts. As of September amendments to Law 42 give prison officials the authority to provide security during transfers, providing an alternate mechanism to transport inmates for court, medical, and other appointments.

The judiciary continued to promote videoconference hearings. Judges were increasingly receptive to using this tool, and during the year the government added several video conference and hearing rooms to prison facilities.

According to judiciary statistics, judicial response time has decreased since the accusatory justice system was implemented--from 278 days to 86 days in the Second Judicial District (Cocle, Veraguas), from 422 days to 18 days in the Third Judicial District (Chiriqui, Bocas del Toro and Comarca Ngabe Bugle), and from 170 days to 60 days in the Fourth Judicial District (Herrera, Los Santos).

Political Prisoners and Detainees

There were no credible reports of political prisoners or detainees. Some individuals detained under corruption charges claimed their charges were politically motivated because they had served under former president Ricardo Martinelli's administration.

Civil Judicial Procedures and Remedies

Citizens have access to the courts to bring lawsuits seeking damages for, or cessation of, human rights violations, although most do not pursue such lawsuits due to the length of the process. There are administrative and judicial remedies for alleged wrongs, and authorities often granted them to citizens who followed through with the process. The court can order civil remedies, including fair compensation to the individual injured. Individuals or organizations may initiate cases involving violations of an individual's human rights by submitting petitions to the IACHR, which in turn may submit the case to the Inter-American Court of Human Rights.

f. Arbitrary or Unlawful Interference with Privacy, Family, Home, or Correspondence

The law prohibits arbitrary interference with privacy, family, home, or correspondence, and the government generally respected these prohibitions.

The law also sets forth requirements for conducting wiretap surveillance. It denies prosecutors authority to order wiretaps on their own and requires judicial oversight.

The investigation of the 2015 illegal wiretapping case against former president Martinelli, as well as against Alejandro Garuz and Gustavo Perez, two former intelligence directors in his administration, continued during the year. In October the Foreign Ministry announced it had formally sought Martinelli's extradition from the United States.

Section 2. Respect for Civil Liberties, Including:

a. Freedom of Speech and Press

The constitution provides for freedom of speech and press. Some journalists complained of harassment, intimidation, and threats when covering stories of impropriety, corruption, or other crimes involving members of the Ministry of Public Security or members of the public security forces.

<u>Press and Media Freedoms</u>: There were reports that the government discouraged journalists from writing stories critical of the administration. According to the Journalists' Union of Panama, as of September the National College of Journalists received 20 complaints of government pressure against media critics.

The Supreme Court upheld the defamation conviction against two *El Panama America* journalists, Jean Marcel Chery and Gustavo Aparicio, for reporting on the 2001 construction of a private road using private funds of former magistrate and minister Winston Spadafora. The court ordered the journalists to pay Spadafora 25,000 balboas ($25,000). Journalistic associations and the local media condemned the ruling as having a chilling effect on media's ability to monitor public servants' financial activities.

During the year the Thirteenth Civil Court ordered daily *La Prensa* to pay brothers David and Daniel Ochy 600,000 balboas ($600,000) for a 2012 case on the grounds of "moral damages." A *La Prensa* publication had reported the Ministry of Public Works favored the Ochys' construction company, TRANSCARIBE Trading, with projects worth millions of dollars.

During the year media outlets controlled by political and business leaders facing legal proceedings claimed those proceedings limited their freedoms of expression. The media outlets continued to publish and broadcast freely throughout the year.

<u>Violence and Harassment</u>: In March journalist Ana Sierra from the *Metro Libre* daily claimed that the security chief of a local hospital intimidated her and forced her to delete photos she had taken of patients she interviewed despite the fact that she had the patients' permission to take the photographs.

Internet Freedom

The government did not restrict or disrupt access to the internet or censor online content, and there were no credible reports the government monitored private online communications without appropriate legal authority.

Forty-eight percent of the population used the internet. Under Law 59 of 2008, the National Authority for Government Innovation provides free, wireless internet in public spaces that reached 86 percent of the population.

Academic Freedom and Cultural Events

There were no government restrictions on academic freedom or cultural events.

b. Freedom of Peaceful Assembly and Association

The law provides for the freedoms of assembly and association, and the government generally respected these rights. Nevertheless, police at times used force to disperse demonstrators, especially when highways or streets were blocked. The law provides for six to 24 months' imprisonment for anyone who, through use of violence, impedes the transit of vehicles on public roads or causes damage to public or private property.

c. Freedom of Religion

See the Department of State's *International Religious Freedom Report* at www.state.gov/religiousfreedomreport/.

d. Freedom of Movement, Internally Displaced Persons, Protection of Refugees, and Stateless Persons

The law provides for freedom of internal movement, foreign travel, emigration, and repatriation, and the government generally respected these rights. The government generally cooperated with the Office of the UN High Commissioner for Refugees (UNHCR) and other humanitarian organizations in providing protection and assistance to refugees, persons under temporary humanitarian protection (THP), asylum seekers, and other persons of concern.

Protection of Refugees

Access to Asylum: The law provides for the granting of asylum or refugee status, and the government has established a system for providing protection to refugees. The process of obtaining refugee status generally took at least a year, but the National Office for the Attention of Refugees (ONPAR) considered expediting cases involving vulnerable applicants, such as pregnant women, minors, and migrants in detention centers.

ONPAR coordinated with the National Migration Service, the Ministry of Labor, UNHCR, the National Civil Registry, and the Colombian embassy to grant legal permanent residency to a Colombian THP group that lived in the Darien region for more than 18 years. The regularization process for those with THP status was completed during the year.

As of September the National Border Protection Force (SENAFRONT) had apprehended 17,306 irregular migrants in the Darien region. While still historically high, apprehensions were down from 31,749 individuals in 2015. Cuban nationals accounted for 5,083 of the migrants. An executive decree allows Cubans who arrive lawfully to receive transit visas without being detained; however, emergency shelters in Paso Canoas housed approximately 3,168 Cuban migrants when Costa Rica closed its border with Panama in February and April. On both occasions, Panama and Mexico reached an agreement to facilitate an "air bridge" for Cuban migrants to fly to Mexico. Cuban migration overland through Panama nearly ended after the government closed its border with Colombia in May.

As of September SENAFRONT also apprehended 7,352 undocumented migrants claiming Congolese nationality whom the government suspected of being Haitian nationals. The government managed camps in the Darien region to provide food, shelter, and medical assistance to the migrants. The government reported continued migrations of persons from South Asia and Africa. Migration authorities opened two new emergency camps in addition to a Roman Catholic-run shelter, where migrants were held for biometric registration before being transferred to the Costa Rica border.

According to UNHCR and its NGO implementing partners, thousands of persons living in the country might be in need of international protection. These included persons in the asylum process, persons not granted asylum, and persons who did not apply for refugee status due to lack of knowledge or fear of deportation.

Employment: Refugees recognized by the authorities have the right to work, but recognized refugees complained that they faced discriminatory hiring practices. In an effort to prevent this discriminatory practice, ONPAR removed the word "refugee" from recognized refugees' identification cards.

All foreigners seeking a work contract must initiate the process through a lawyer and pay a government fee of 700 balboas ($700) to obtain a work permit that expires upon termination of the labor contract or after one year, whichever comes first.

<u>Access to Basic Services</u>: Education authorities sometimes denied refugees access to education, while refusing to issue diplomas to others if they could not present school records from their country of origin. The Ministry of Education enforced the government's 2015 decree requiring schools to accept students in the asylum process at the grade level commensurate with the applicants' prior studies.

<u>Durable Solutions</u>: The law allows persons legally recognized as refugees or with asylum status who have lived in the country for more than three years to seek permanent residency.

The government generally permitted freedom of movement for recognized refugees and asylum seekers.

Section 3. Freedom to Participate in the Political Process

The law provides citizens the ability to choose their government in free and fair periodic elections held by secret ballot based on universal and equal suffrage. The law provides for direct popular election every five years of the president, vice president, legislators, and local representatives. Naturalized citizens may not hold specified categories of elective office, such as the presidency.

Elections and Political Participation

<u>Recent Elections</u>: In May 2014 voters chose Juan Carlos Varela Rodriguez, the candidate of the opposition party, The People First Alliance, as president in national elections independent observers considered generally free and fair. Elected at the same time were 71 national legislators, 77 mayors, 648 local representatives, and seven council members.

<u>Political Parties and Political Participation</u>: The law requires new political parties to meet strict membership and organizational standards to gain official recognition and participate in national campaigns. The law also requires that political parties obtain the equivalent of 4 percent of the total votes cast to maintain legal standing. The Revolutionary Democratic Party, Panamenista Party, Democratic Change Party, and Popular Party all complied with the requirement. In July the Broad Front for Democracy gathered more than 57,000 petition signatures in support of its registration as a party, short of the 74,000 needed to regain legal recognition following its failure to obtain 4 percent of the vote in the 2014 election. The Electoral Tribunal also oversees internal party elections.

<u>Participation of Women and Minorities</u>: Women participated in political life on the same basis as men. Women represented 12 of 71 members in the National Assembly, 1 of 9 Supreme Court Justices, and 12 of 40 cabinet level officials, including the vice president and vice ministers.

Five seats in the legislature are designated to represent the country's recognized indigenous regions. Afro-Panamanians make up a majority of the country's ethnic minorities. There were three Afro-Panamanians on the Supreme Court and nine Afro-Panamanian deputies in the National Assembly; no Afro-Panamanians served in the cabinet or in any other high-level government positions.

Section 4. Corruption and Lack of Transparency in Government

The law provides criminal penalties for corruption by officials, and the government generally implemented these laws effectively; however, there were allegations that government officials and members of the previous government administration engaged in corrupt practices with impunity. Corruption remained a problem in the executive, judicial, and legislative branches as well as in the security forces.

Anticorruption mechanisms such as asset forfeiture, whistleblower, and witness protection, plea bargaining, and professional conflict-of-interest rules exist.

<u>Corruption</u>: The National Authority for Transparency and Access to Public Information (ANTAI) combats and investigates government corruption. During the year there were several credible allegations of corruption against current or former members of the government.

In March the government established the High Level Secretariat to Prevent Corruption (SEPRECO) to improve transparency. As a pilot program under ANTAI's authority, SEPRECO was tasked with preventing corruption in public bids and payment of bribes and protecting foreign investment.

In April, the Tenth District Penal judge sentenced a former Social Security Fund finance and managing director, Alberto Maggiori, to eight years in prison for embezzlement in awarding two linked companies contracts of more than two million dollars in 2011 and 2012. Maggiori also faced criminal charges in a different corruption case.

The anticorruption prosecutor continued the investigation of Panama Canal Authority board member Lourdes Castillo, her business partner Samuel Israel, and his wife Alexandra de Israel, for alleged payment of bribes in 2014 in exchange for a contract with the Panama Maritime Authority (AMP). Former president Martinelli approved a contract for Pele System without its participation in the bidding process. The new administration filed a complaint based on an alleged overpayment of 12 million balboas ($12 million) to Pele System. The anticorruption prosecutor's investigation found that Pele System made payments to Castillo and the Israel couple's businesses incorporated in the British Virgin Islands.

Corruption and a lack of accountability among the police continued to be a problem, though the government took steps to address violations. Thirty-two agents were dismissed on corruption grounds and were under investigation by the Public Ministry. The agents included a police captain and a lieutenant arrested in August along with 11 others for allegedly falsifying prisoners' records and altering criminal sentences as well as former civilian agents from the penitentiary system who allegedly charged up to 70,000 balboas ($70,000) to assist gang members to leave prison early.

To address police corruption at the prisons, the 2015 PNP policy requiring members of the PNP who serve as prison guards to rotate to other police functions after two years continued. The policy aims to reduce corrupt behavior by preventing PNP guards from remaining at one prison for an extended period; the PNP also began to provide a monthly bonus of 35 balboas ($35) for each agent assigned to the prisons to reduce incentives for corruption.

The case against former minister of labor Alma Cortes related to charges of illicit enrichment continued. The prosecutor claimed Cortes could not justify how she accrued two million dollars in assets and bank accounts while serving as minister of labor. Cortes was detained in August.

In August, ANTAI opened an investigation regarding AMP Director General Jorge Barakat's alleged receipt of basketball game tickets valued at more than 1,000 balboas ($1,000) from an AMP contractor; he attended the game during an official trip.

In August the former Agriculture Institute director general under the current administration, Edwin Cardenas, was detained under charges of mismanagement of more than six million dollars of public funds. The fourth anticorruption prosecutor charged Cardenas for wrongdoings from July 2014 through April 2015.

<u>Financial Disclosure</u>: The law requires certain executive and judiciary officials to submit a financial disclosure statement to the Comptroller General's Office. The information is not made public unless the official grants permission for access to the public.

<u>Public Access to Information</u>: The law provides for public access to information about public entities, with the exception of cabinet meeting minutes. Public procurement notices are posted online. ANTAI statistics as of July showed 24 of 43 new requests for access to information had been fulfilled; the others remained pending as of August. Citizens can appeal denials of information to the Supreme Court. Deadlines are 30 days, and there are no processing fees. There are sanctions, primarily fines, for noncompliance.

Section 5. Governmental Attitude Regarding International and Nongovernmental Investigation of Alleged Violations of Human Rights

A number of domestic and international human rights groups generally operated without government restriction, investigating and publishing their findings on human rights cases. Government officials generally were cooperative and responsive to their views. In November the country hosted a session of the IACHR.

<u>Government Human Rights Bodies</u>: The ombudsman, elected by the National Assembly, has moral but not legal authority, received government cooperation, and operated without government or party interference. The Ombudsman's Office referred cases to the proper investigating authorities. The central government approved five million dollars instead of the seven million dollars requested for the office's 2017 budget. In March a human rights activist and former foreign policy director general at the Foreign Affairs Ministry, Alfredo Castillero Hoyos, was elected as the new ombudsman for a five-year term.

Section 6. Discrimination, Societal Abuses, and Trafficking in Persons

Women

<u>Rape and Domestic Violence</u>: The law criminalizes rape, including spousal rape, with prison terms of five to 10 years, or eight to 10 years under aggravating circumstances, such as use of a weapon. The government generally implemented criminal aspects of the law better than protection aspects of the law. Rapes constituted the majority of sexual crimes investigated by the PNP and its

Directorate of Judicial Investigation. NGOs reported that many women were reluctant to report rapes due to fear of retaliation, perceived low likelihood of a response, and social stigma.

The law against gender violence stipulates stiff penalties for harassment and both physical and emotional abuse and provides for prison terms of up to 30 years for murder. Officials and civil society organizations agreed that domestic violence continued to be a serious and underreported crime. Statistics varied widely between reporting authorities, as prosecutorial discretion contributed to an uneven application of laws and statistics surrounding domestic violence.

The Ombudsman's Office continued its program "Mujer Conoce tus Derechos" (Woman, Know Your Rights), which included a wide distribution of flyers featuring women of different ages, professions and ethnic groups, with a quotation expressing their views on gender problems.

There is a lack of shelters for victims of domestic abuse. The government, through the National Institute for Women Affairs, operated a shelter in Panama City for victims of domestic abuse and offered social, psychological, medical, and legal services.

Sexual Harassment: The law prohibits sexual harassment in cases of employer-employee relations in the public and private sectors and in teacher-student relations. Violators face a maximum three-year prison sentence. The extent of the problem was difficult to determine, because convictions for sexual harassment were rare, and pre-employment sexual harassment was not actionable. The lack of formal reports was attributable to the absence of a follow-up protocol after initial complaints are filed, the difficulty of providing proof in the absence of third-party witnesses, the lack of favorable results in the few past cases, and the likelihood a woman filing a complaint would be fired.

Reproductive Rights: Couples and individuals generally have the right to decide the number, spacing, and timing of their children and manage their reproductive health; they also have access to the information and means to do so, free from discrimination, coercion, or violence. The law provides for medical professionals to perform abortions only in the case of danger to the fetus or to the mother.

Discrimination: The law prohibits discrimination based on gender, and women enjoyed the same legal status and rights as men. The law recognizes joint property in marriages. The law mandates equal pay for men and women in equivalent jobs.

The Ministry of Social Development and the National Institute of Women promoted equality of women in the workplace and equal pay for equal work, attempted to reduce sexual harassment, and advocated legal reforms. Although an illegal hiring practice, some employers continued to request pregnancy tests.

Children

Birth Registration: The law provides citizenship for all persons born in the country, but parents of children born in remote areas sometimes had difficulty obtaining birth registration certificates. The National Secretariat for Children, Adolescents, and the Family estimated the registration level of births at 92 percent.

Child Abuse: The Ministry of Social Development (MIDES) maintained a free hotline for children and adults to report child abuse and advertised it widely. The ministry provided funding to children's shelters operated by NGOs in seven provinces and continued a program that used pamphlets in schools to sensitize teachers, children, and parents about mistreatment and sexual abuse of children.

Early and Forced Marriage: The minimum legal age for marriage is 18. The government prohibits early marriage even with parental permission.

Sexual Exploitation of Children: Officials continued to prosecute cases of sexual abuse of children in urban and rural areas, as well as within indigenous communities. Officials believed that commercial sexual exploitation of children occurred, including in tourist areas in Panama City and in beach communities, although they did not keep separate statistics.

International Child Abductions: The country is a party to the 1980 Hague Convention on the Civil Aspects of International Child Abduction. See the Department of State's *Annual Report on International Child Abduction* at travel.state.gov/content/childabduction/en/legal/compliance.html.

Anti-Semitism

Jewish community leaders estimated there were 15,000 Jews in the country. There were no known reports of anti-Semitic acts.

Trafficking in Persons

See the Department of State's *Trafficking in Persons Report* at
www.state.gov/j/tip/rls/tiprpt/.

Persons with Disabilities

The law prohibits discrimination based on physical, sensory, intellectual, or mental
disabilities in employment, education, air travel and other transportation, access to
health care, the judicial system, and the provision of other state services; however,
the constitution permits the denial of naturalization to persons with mental or
physical disabilities. The law mandates access to new or remodeled public
buildings for persons with disabilities and requires that schools integrate children
with disabilities. Despite provisions of the law, persons with disabilities
experienced discrimination in a number of these areas.

Panama City's bus fleet was not wheelchair accessible. Metro elevators were
frequently locked and could not be used. A lack of ramps further limited access to
the stations. Most businesses had wheelchair ramps and accessible parking spaces
as required by law, but in many cases they did not meet the government's size
specifications.

Some public schools admitted children with mental and physical disabilities, but
most did not have adequate facilities for children with disabilities.

In April the Ombudsman's Office submitted a complaint against a public junior
high school for not providing an appropriate curriculum to a 16-year-old student
with learning disabilities. As of August the Ministry of Education Integration
Directorate had not resolved the issue, and the teenager continued to miss school.

Few private schools admitted children with disabilities. The high costs of hiring
professional tutors to accompany children to private schools--a requirement of all
private schools--burdened parents of students with disabilities.

The government-sponsored Guardian Angel program continued to provide a
monthly subsidy of 80 balboas ($80) for children with significant physical
disabilities. To qualify, the parents or guardian of a child must be living in poverty
and must submit a medical certification specifying the degree of the disability and
the child's dependency on another person. Authorities conducted home visits to
ensure the beneficiaries' guardians used the funds for the intended purpose.

As of March the National Secretariat for the Social Integration of Persons with Disabilities (SENADIS) had issued 324 new certifications that, in the form of an identification card, allowed persons with disabilities to receive discounts on medications, health services, utilities, transportation, and entertainment. Recipients reported that private medical facilities and pharmacies honored the discounts but that entertainment establishments lacked awareness about the certifications.

In May, President Varela signed Law 15 to expand the rights of persons with disabilities. The law establishes that disability issues are not only a matter of public health but also a human rights concern. It mandates the government to coordinate internally to assign more program funds to disabilities issues, to provide timely medical attention to persons with disabilities and to waive import taxes on medical equipment.

In June the Ministry of Labor provided job-skills training to persons with disabilities. As of September, 59 local companies reportedly hired 64 persons with disabilities through Ministry of Labor-sponsored job fairs.

SENADIS continued to operate the Family Businesses Project, which assisted low-income families with members with disabilities to start microbusinesses. By July the government provided 50 balboas ($50) per month to 59 new beneficiaries. Throughout the year the government also donated rehabilitation equipment to low-income persons with disabilities.

National/Racial/Ethnic Minorities

Minority groups were generally integrated into mainstream society. Prejudice was directed, however, at recent immigrants and the Afro-Panamanian community. Cultural and language differences and immigration status hindered the integration of immigrant and first-generation individuals from China, India, and the Middle East into mainstream society. Additionally, some members of these communities were themselves reluctant to integrate into mainstream society.

The Afro-Panamanian community continued to be underrepresented in positions of political and economic power. Areas where they lived conspicuously lacked government services and social investment. In October the National Assembly passed a bill to create a National Secretariat for the Development of Afro-Panamanians to focus on social and economic advancement of that minority group.

The bill also provides for a mechanism for the secretariat to work with the national census to ensure an accurate count of Afro-descendant residents in the country.

The law prohibits discrimination in access to public accommodations such as restaurants, stores, and other privately owned establishments; few complaints were filed. The Ombudsman's Office intervened in several cases before students with Rastafarian braids were permitted entry into public school classrooms.

There were reports of racial discrimination against various ethnic groups in the workplace (see section 7.d.). Lighter-skinned persons continued to be disproportionately represented in management positions and jobs that required dealing with the public, such as bank tellers and receptionists.

The terms for board members of the National Council for the Afro Ethnic Group, an organization created in 2005 by an executive decree to combat discrimination against Afro-Panamanians, expired, and they did not have successors as of August. The government appointed a paid manager to work for the council, but the national coordinator reported a lack of communication between the manager, the council, and the national coordinator for the country's black organizations.

Indigenous People

The law affords indigenous persons the same political and legal rights as other citizens, protects their ethnic identity and native languages, and requires the government to provide bilingual literacy programs in indigenous communities. Indigenous individuals have the legal right to take part in decisions affecting their lands, cultures, traditions, and the allocation and exploitation of natural resources. Nevertheless, they continued to be marginalized. Traditional community leaders governed legally designated areas for five of the country's seven indigenous groups. The government did not recognize such areas for the smaller Bri Bri and Naso communities. In June companies building a dam project signed an agreement with Ngabe communities to resume the construction of 26 housing units to be used to resettle residents from the dam area following the IACHR's review of the case.

There were multiple conflicts between the government and indigenous groups regarding decisions affecting indigenous land and autonomy. In April the Guna General Congress declared in a letter to President Varela that it was breaking relations with the Panamanian government. Guna authorities also demanded that the National Migration Service and the Maritime Authority vacate their offices inside the Guna Yala comarca. Guna leaders claimed the Maritime Authority's ruling in favor of an Austrian tourist who refused to pay tax for using scuba gear in a prohibited area of the comarca represented government interference with indigenous autonomy. Also in April the National Assembly approved a law establishing the right of indigenous groups to public consultation and free and informed consent of legislative and administrative measures, programs, and plans that affect their collective rights. The Supreme Court also voided a 2010 executive decree, which allowed traditional authorities of the Ngabe Bugle to choose their electoral system.

The Ngabe Bugle and the Naso continued to clash with the government over the issue of hydroelectric plants on territorial lands, including over the Barro Blanco dam project, which would flood approximately 14 acres of "annexed lands," as well as submerge a pre-Columbian petroglyph that practitioners of the main Ngabe Bugle religion, Mama Tatda, worship. In May the government's support of Generadora del Istmo, S.A.'s (GENISA) conducting a test fill of the Barro Blanco dam reservoir resulted in a wave of protests in the Ngabe Bugle comarca and Panama City that briefly closed major highways and resulted in the arrests of several protest leaders. In late August the government signed an agreement with the Ngabe Bugle leader to place GENISA as the plant operator; allocate 50 percent of the jobs created by the project to indigenous workers; and terminate all other concessions on the Tabasara River, with future concessions within the region to be approved by a plenary of Ngabe Bugle congresses at the local, regional and supraregional level.

The Ngabe Bugle people in the area of Bocas del Toro also protested against the Chan 2 thermoelectric projects and demanded their cancellation.

Although the country's law is the ultimate authority in indigenous comarcas, many indigenous persons misunderstood their rights and, due to their inadequate command of the Spanish language, failed to employ legal channels when threatened.

Societal and employment discrimination against indigenous persons was widespread. Employers frequently did not afford indigenous workers basic rights provided by law, such as a minimum wage, social security benefits, termination pay, and job security. Laborers on the country's sugar, coffee, and banana plantations (the majority of whom were indigenous persons) continued to work in overcrowded and unsanitary conditions. Employers were less likely to provide adequate housing or food to indigenous migrant laborers, and indigenous children were much more likely to work long hours of farm labor than nonindigenous children (see section 7.d.). The Ministry of Labor conducted limited oversight of working conditions in remote areas.

Education continued to be deficient in the comarcas, especially beyond the primary grades. There were not enough teachers in these remote and inaccessible areas, with many multigrade schools often poorly constructed and lacking running water. In April the government began a project to eliminate "escuelas rancho" (rural impoverished schools) with an overall budget of 100 million balboas ($100 million). Access to health care was a significant problem in the indigenous comarcas, as reflected in high rates of maternal and infant mortality and malnutrition. The government continued to invest in transport infrastructure by repairing roads in the comarca to improve access to basic services.

Acts of Violence, Discrimination, and Other Abuses Based on Sexual Orientation and Gender Identity

The law does not prohibit discrimination based on sexual orientation, and there was societal discrimination based on sexual orientation and gender identity, which often led to denial of employment opportunities (see section 7.d.).

The PNP's internal regulations describe homosexual conduct by its employees as an offense. Harassment of lesbian, gay, bisexual, transgender, and intersex (LGBTI) persons by security forces was a major complaint of the New Men and Women of Panama, the main LGBTI organization, but formal complaints were rare due to the perception that the reports were not taken seriously or that complaints could be used against claimants in the absence of nondiscrimination legislation. On July 2 gay rights advocates organized and participated without impediment in the 12th annual gay pride parade. Panama City Mayor Jose Blandon and his family led the march for the second consecutive year with a record attendance of 4,000 participants.

The country does not recognize any relationship between LGBTI partners in terms of health care, parental rights, property rights, or any publicly provided services.

In August a homemade video showing a mother physically abusing her minor son for his alleged homosexual tendencies went viral. With the public's assistance, the National Secretariat for Children Issues (SENNIAF) identified the mother and took her into custody, but a SENNIAF official angered LGBTI groups when referring to the minor's alleged homosexual tendency as a "deviation" on national television.

HIV and AIDS Social Stigma

The law prohibits discrimination against persons with HIV/AIDS in employment and education, but discrimination continued to be common due to ignorance of the law and a lack of mechanisms for ensuring compliance. The 2015 MIDES National Network for the Continued Integral Attention of Persons with HIV/AIDS continued during the year. MIDES collaborated with NGO PROBIDSIDA to conduct HIV/AIDS outreach to students in public junior and high schools. During the year PROBIDSIDA also worked with the Ministry of Public Security "Barrios Seguros" program to provide HIV/AIDS training and free testing services to at-risk youth from vulnerable communities. Youth who tested positive received medical treatment.

LGBTI citizens reported mistreatment by health-care workers, including unnecessary quarantines. PROBIDSIDA reported a case of discrimination, whereby co-workers did not want to work with an HIV-positive employee, resulting in his transfer to multiple departments. As of August PROBIDSIDA was working with health authorities to resolve the case.

Section 7. Worker Rights

a. Freedom of Association and the Right to Collective Bargaining

The law provides for the right of private-sector workers to form and join unions of their choice subject to the union's registration with the government. Public servants may not form unions but may form associations that can bargain collectively on behalf of members.

The law provides for the right of private-sector workers to strike. The Administrative Career Law grants public-sector employees the same right when the strike has been deemed legal and when a minimum percentage of workers cover essential positions, as set out in the law. The right to strike does not apply in areas deemed vital to public welfare and security, including the police. The law provides all private sector and public-sector workers the right to bargain collectively, prohibits employer antiunion discrimination, and protects workers engaged in union activities from loss of employment or discriminatory transfers. It requires reinstatement of workers terminated for union activity.

The law places several restrictions on these rights, including requiring Panamanian citizenship to serve on a trade union's executive board, requiring a minimum of 40 persons to form a private-sector union (either by company across trades or by trade across companies), and permitting only one trade union per business establishment. The International Labor Organization (ILO) continued to criticize the 40-person minimum as too large for workers wanting to form a union within a company; Panamanian unions, as well as the government and private sector, reiterated their support for keeping the figure at 40 individuals.

Fifty public servants are required to form a worker's association. Member associations represent public-sector workers such as doctors, nurses, firefighters, and administrative staff in government ministries. The law stipulates there may not be more than one association in a public-sector institution and permits no more than one chapter per province.

In the private sector, the Labor Code provides that if the government does not respond to a registration application within 15 days, the union automatically gains legal recognition. In the public sector, unions gain legal recognition automatically if the General Directorate for Administrative Public Sector Careers does not respond to registration applications within 30 days.

A majority of employees must support a strike, which must be related to improvement of working conditions, a collective bargaining agreement, or in support of another strike of workers on the same project (solidarity strike). In the event of a strike, at least 20 to 30 percent of the workforce must continue to provide minimum services, particularly public services as defined by the law, such as transportation, sanitation, mail delivery, hospital care, telecommunications, and public availability of essential foodstuffs.

Strikes in essential transportation services are limited to those involving public passenger services. The law prohibits strikes for the Panama Canal Authority's employees but allows unions to organize and bargain collectively on such issues as schedules and safety. It also provides for arbitration to resolve disputes. By law the National Federation of Public Servants (FENASEP), an umbrella federation of 21 public-sector worker associations, is not permitted to call strikes or negotiate collective bargaining agreements. Individual associations under FENASEP may negotiate on behalf of their members. FENASEP leaders noted that collective bargaining claims were heard and recognized, but they reported a lack of changes afterwards, particularly regarding firings without cause. FENASEP discussed structural changes with President Varela to promote equity and provide adequate treatment of the public sector as a sector with established rights like that of unionized groups. During the year FENASEP focused on the following problems:

the lack of job stability, the lack of a policy for salary beyond the minimum wage, salary gap and equal pay for men and women, and the lack of indemnity pay for unjustified firings.

Supreme Court decisions recognize that collective agreements negotiated between employers and unorganized workers have legal status equivalent to collective bargaining agreements negotiated by unions. Executive decrees provide that an employer may not enter into collective negotiations with nonunionized workers when a union exists and that a preexisting agreement with nonunionized workers cannot be used to refuse to negotiate with unionized workers. The labor ministry's *Manual of Labor Rights and Obligations* provides that unorganized workers may petition the ministry regarding labor rights violations and may exercise the right to strike.

An executive decree protects employees from employer interference in labor rights, specifically including "employer-directed unions," and mandates that workers be able to choose unions freely, without penalty.

Since the beginning of the Varela administration in July 2014, the government approved more than 20 applications it received for union formations and denied two based on evidence of company owners' influence. The three main focal points for Ministry of Labor during the year were to create jobs, to ensure that persons with disabilities had access to the workforce, and to address unjustified firings and payment of back salaries owed to workers.

In addition to the court system, the Conciliation Board of the labor ministry has the authority to resolve certain labor disagreements, such as internal union disputes, enforcement of the minimum wage, and some dismissal issues. The law allows arbitration by mutual consent, at the request of the employee or the ministry in case of a collective dispute in a public service company. It allows either party to appeal if arbitration is mandated during a collective dispute in a public-service company. The separate Labor Foundation's Tripartite Conciliation Board has sole competency for disputes related to domestic employees, some dismissal issues, and claims of less than 1,500 balboas ($1,500).

For public-sector workers, the Board of Appeal and Conciliation in the Ministry of the Presidency hears and resolves complaints. The board refers complaints it cannot resolve to an arbitral tribunal, which consists of representatives from the employer, the worker's association, and a third member chosen by the first two. Tribunal decisions are final.

The government and employers generally respected freedom of association and the right to collective bargaining; however, the inspections and notifications departments lacked funding and inspectors to adequately enforce labor laws. Employers often hired employees under short-term contracts to avoid paying benefits that accrue to long-term employees. Article 222, Item 1, of the Labor Code states that employers have the right to dismiss any employee without justifiable cause before the two-year tenure term. As a result employers frequently hired workers for one year and 11 months and subsequently laid them off to circumvent laws that make firing employees more difficult after two years of employment. This practice is illegal if the same employee is rehired as a temporary worker after being laid off, although employees rarely reported the practice.

b. Prohibition of Forced or Compulsory Labor

The law prohibits all forms of forced labor of adults or children. The law establishes penalties of 15 to 20 years' imprisonment for forced labor involving movement (either cross-border or within the country) and six to 10 years' imprisonment for forced labor not involving movement.

While prostitution is legal, according to media reports, forced labor continued to be a problem in the commercial sex industry, often due to disputes between women and their employers over wage amounts agreed in oral contracts.

Also, see the Department of State's *Trafficking in Persons Report* at www.state.gov/j/tip/rls/tiprpt/.

c. Prohibition of Child Labor and Minimum Age for Employment

The law prohibits the employment of children under age 14, although children who have not completed primary school may not begin work until age 15. Article 716 of the Family Code permits children ages 12 to 14 to perform domestic and agricultural work as regulated by the Labor Code with regard to schedule, salary, contract, and type. Article 119 of the Labor Code allows children ages 12 to 15 to perform light work in agriculture if the work is outside regular school hours. Article 123 of the Labor Code allows children over the age of 12 to perform light domestic work and says employers must ensure the child attends school through primary school. The law does not limit the total number of hours these children may work or define what kinds of light work children may perform. The law prohibits 14- to 18-year-old children from engaging in potentially hazardous work such as work with electrical energy, explosives, or flammable, toxic, and radioactive substances; work underground and on railroads, airplanes, and boats; and work in nightclubs, bars, and casinos. In January the Ministry of Labor updated the list of hazardous occupations and established a minimum age of 14 for minors enrolled in training programs to perform activities designated as hazardous provided these activities are carried out in accordance with conditions prescribed by the appropriate authority and after consultation with worker and employer organizations.

Youths under age 16 may work no more than six hours per day or 36 hours per week, while those 16 and 17 may work no more than seven hours per day or 42 hours per week. Children under 18 may not work between 6 p.m. and 8 a.m.

The Ministry of Labor (MITRADEL) generally enforced the law effectively in the formal sector, enforcing child labor provisions in response to complaints and ordering the termination of unauthorized employees. It did not do so in the informal economy. By law violators can be fined up to 700 balboas ($700) for a first-time violation. Employers who endanger the physical or mental health of a child may face two to six years' imprisonment. The law includes punishment of up to 12 years' imprisonment for anyone who recruits children under age 18 or uses them to participate actively in armed hostilities.

In April, MITRADEL and Consejo Nacional de la Empresa (CONEP) signed an agreement of cooperation wherein they formed an alliance to eradicate child labor by 2020. MITRADEL and CONEP will establish a series of joint programs to prevent and eradicate child labor in Panama through actions and activities within public policies, awareness raising, and job training for adolescents.

During the year MITRADEL, through its Anti-Child Labor and Protection of Adolescent Workers division (DIRETIPAT), launched a new program called Planting Values for the Future. Under this program, DIRETIPAT publicly recognized 18 companies that offer paid internship programs designed for adolescents. DIRETIPAT follows the standards of Panamanian law and ILO recommendations in assessing the internship programs.

The National Office for Children, Youth, and Family implemented programs to identify children engaged in the worst forms of child labor, to remove them from exploitative situations, and to provide them with services. The Ministry of Labor offered training on the topic of child labor and lessons learned to various stakeholders.

The government ratified ILO Convention 189 Concerning Decent Work for Domestic Workers and adopted a policy framework on the elimination of child labor in domestic work. The Committee for the Eradication of Child Labor and the Protection of Adolescent Workers also updated the Roadmap towards the Elimination of Child Labor, and outlined interagency action plans and budgets for 2016-19. Furthermore, the Ministry of Education began structural improvements to 1,000 schools in indigenous areas, where there was a high prevalence of child labor.

Also, see the Department of Labor's *Findings on the Worst Forms of Child Labor* at www.dol.gov/ilab/reports/child-labor/findings/.

d. Discrimination with Respect to Employment and Occupation

Labor laws and regulations prohibit discrimination regarding race, gender, religion, political opinion, citizenship, disability, language, social status, HIV status and other communicable diseases, but they do not do so on the basis of sexual orientation, and/or gender identity.

Discrimination in employment and occupation occurred with respect to race, sex, gender, disability, sexual orientation and/or gender identity, and HIV-positive status (see section 6). Discrimination against migrant workers also occurred (see section 6).

e. Acceptable Conditions of Work

The minimum hourly wage for private sector employees ranged from 1.46 balboas ($1.46) to 4.18 balboas ($4.18), depending on the region and sector. Working 45 hours per week, a worker would receive monthly earnings between 285 balboas ($285) to 815 balboas ($815). Public servants received a monthly minimum wage of 500 balboas ($500). The monthly poverty line was 98 balboas ($98) in rural areas and 131 balboas ($131) in urban areas. Food and the use of housing facilities were considered part of the salary for some workers, such as domestic and agricultural workers. Minimum monthly salaries for domestic workers ranged from 225 balboas ($225) to 250 balboas ($250). The agricultural sector and the marine and aviation sectors received the lowest and highest minimum wages, respectively.

The law establishes a standard workweek of 48 hours, provides for at least one 24-hour rest period weekly, limits the number of hours worked per week, provides for premium pay for overtime, and prohibits compulsory overtime. There is no annual limit on the total number of overtime hours allowed. If employees work more than three hours of overtime in one day or more than nine overtime hours in a week, excess overtime hours must be paid at an additional 75 percent above the normal wage. Workers have the right to 30 days' paid vacation for every 11 months of continuous work, including those who do not work full time. The Ministry of Labor is responsible for setting health and safety standards. Standards set were generally current and appropriate for the main industries in the country. The Labor Code requires employers to provide a safe workplace environment, including the provision of protective clothing and equipment for workers.

The Ministry of Labor generally enforced these standards in the formal sector. The inspection office comprises two groups: the Panama City-based headquarters group and the regional group. As of November within the headquarters there were 34 inspectors reported, including nine general labor inspectors, four child labor inspectors, and 12 safety inspectors in the construction industry. The construction industry paid the salaries of construction industry inspectors, although the inspectors remained ministry employees. The regional branches had 55 inspectors. As of September the Ministry of Labor had conducted labor inspections nationwide. Allowable fines for violations were low--often between 25 balboas ($25) and 500 balboas ($500)--and generally insufficient to deter violations. During the year, however, the government levied fines according to the number of workers affected, resulting in larger overall fines. The ministry had issued fines for migration violations, for safety and security violations, for general labor issues violations, and for violations related to child labor.

Inspectors from the Ministry of Labor and the occupational health section of the Social Security Administration reported conducting periodic inspections of hazardous employment sites. The law requires the resident engineer and a ministry construction industry inspector to remain on construction sites, establish fines for noncompliance, and identify a tripartite group composed of the Chamber of Construction, SUNTRACS (the largest union of construction workers in the country), and the ministry to regulate adherence.

Most workers formally employed in urban areas earned the minimum wage or more. Approximately 40 percent of the working population worked in the informal sector, and many earned well below the minimum wage. In most rural areas, unskilled laborers, including street vendors and those involved in forestry, fishing, and handicraft production, earned three to six dollars per day without benefits. The Ministry of Labor was less likely to enforce labor laws in most rural areas (see section 6, Indigenous People).

Some construction workers and their employers were occasionally lax about basic safety measures, frequently due to their perception that it reduced productivity. Equipment was often outdated, broken, or lacking safety devices, due in large part to a fear that the replacement cost would be prohibitive.

Workers could not remove themselves from situations that endangered health or safety without jeopardy to their employment, and authorities did not effectively protect workers in this situation.

www.ingramcontent.com/pod-product-compliance
Lightning Source LLC
Chambersburg PA
CBHW080819280726
48660CB00018B/3538